J*STEELHEAD* JIG FISHING
Techniques & Tackle

Dave Vedder
and Drew Harthorn

Frank **A**mato PORTLAND

Published in 1996 by Frank Amato
Publications, Inc.
P.O. Box 82112
Portland, Oregon 97282
(503) 653-8108

ISBN: 1-57188-073-9
UPC: 0-81127-00101-9

Book Design: Charlie Clifford

Printed in Singapore
10 9 8 7 6 5 4 3 2

Contents

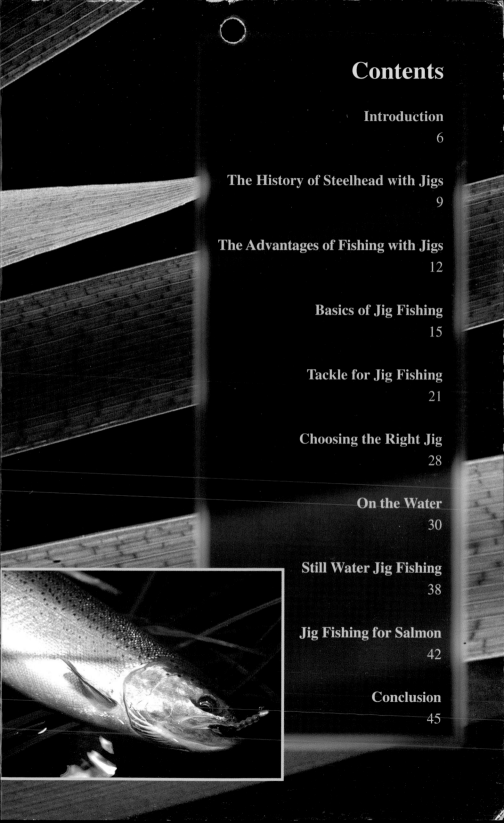

Drew Harthorn

A lifelong Northwest resident, Drew Harthorn began to appreciate everything that the outdoors had to offer at an early age. His field of expertise is fishing, both freshwater and saltwater.

Drew has traveled in search of fishing opportunities from Alaska to the west coast of Mexico and all points between. His favorite types of fish are the Pacific salmon and steelhead. He also fishes for various rock fish and Pacific halibut, but it's the steelhead that holds his main interest. As a licensed Washington state guide, he favors the Olympic Peninsula rivers to get his steelhead fix.

Since 1990 Drew has written the weekly fishing column for the Bremerton *Sun* which appears on the Thursday Outdoors page. He has also written for various outdoor magazines.

Drew field tests and helps develop new products for several tackle companies, including Beau Mac Enterprises—steelhead and salmon tackle, Dr. Juice—artificial lures and attractant scents and Ande Monofilament—fishing line. Drew also gives fishing lectures at the outdoor and boat shows, which consist of slide presentations and a hands-on, how-to segments.

Dave Vedder

Dave Vedder was born and raised in western Washington. His family started taking him salmon fishing at Sekiu while he was still in diapers. From his teenage years to the present, Dave has been a fishing addict. His love of fishing has taken him from Alaska to Africa and from Canada to Cuba, but his first love remains the streams and rivers of the Northwest.

In 1986 Dave began writing to share his angling experiences with others who love fish and fishing as much as he does. Over the years he has had the pleasure of travelling to many rivers all over North America and fishing with some of the continent's finest anglers and best companions. Dave's first book *Float Fishing for Steelhead* has been well received. Many anglers have called and written to tell how much they enjoyed using the techniques described in that book.

Travels to Canada taught Dave the effectiveness of float fishing. Expert anglers like Drew Harthorn and Nick Amato taught him how effective jigs can be when fished beneath a float. He now fishes almost exclusively with floats and uses jigs beneath his floats whenever possible. He hopes this book will help others enjoy the thrill of hooking more steelhead with this effective and exciting technique.

Drew Harthorn and Dave Vedder, longtime angling chums, pose with a jig-caught Olympic Peninsula chum salmon.

Introduction

Dave Vedder

This is essentially a how-to book. As such, it will strive to answer four of the five essential questions of journalism: What, where, who, when and why. It is here that we attempt to answer the fifth question—why. There are actually two separate "why" questions that need to be answered. The first is why should you learn yet another method of steelhead and salmon fishing? This question, I am confident, we can answer to your satisfaction. The second "why" question has to do with our reasons for writing this book. That is a much more complicated question. Partially, because I will need to speak for the co-author, Drew Harthorn, and partially because I need to answer for my own motivations which are not always altogether clear, even to me. I am after all a steelheader—one of nature's strangest and most quixotic creatures.

The short answer to the question of why you should embrace a new method of steelheading and river salmon fishing is because it works and works very well. Any experienced angler knows that there is no one lure or bait which always works best for steelhead and salmon. Fish, river conditions and the types of holding water fish occupy are too varied and complex for any one bait or lure to always be the best choice. I am thankful that is so. Steelheading would lose much of its spark if we all chose to fish the same lure in the same way every day. Part of the spirit of our sport is the sense of exploration and adventure that accompanies trying new techniques to trick the fish.

Jigs will not always out-perform every other weapon in the steelheader's arsenal. But they consistently take salmon and steelhead under varied conditions, and often work wonders when all other tricks fail. I know this is true, and I suspect you may believe it as well. You wouldn't have read this far if you didn't.

Steelhead Jig Fishing is intended to give you the information you need to successfully fish jigs under a large variety of conditions. It will also give you the confidence to fish jigs in preference over other lures and baits. Drew and I know that you must have faith in jigs before you will give them a chance to show their stuff.

Like most other steelheaders, I was slow to give jigs a try. I had found my share of success with plastic baits, such as Gooey Bobs, Jensen Eggs and pink worms. When those failed me, I grudgingly switched to natural baits such as sand shrimp, salmon eggs or prawns. When fishing with friends who owned boats, I would try pulling plugs—a steelheading method that I found as boring as it is effective. I saw no reason to find another pocket in my vest for these strange looking lead-head jigs some people claimed to use with great success. Then some of the best steelheaders I know began telling me about phenomenal successes with jigs.

Nick Amato was the first to give me an account of how deadly jigs can be when conditions are less than ideal. He called me on a January day when we had been suffering through a long stretch of cold weather. The rivers were dead low, and the water temperature was in the thirties. No one was having much luck on the steelhead scene. Yet Nick was so excited I had to ask him to slow down as he told me about one of the most amazing steelheading experiences I had ever heard. He and Rich Paradzinski had fished a deep pool on the Sandy River. Twelve other anglers had been working the pool with every possible combination of steelhead gear when Rich and Nick arrived. They used small floats, light line and one-eighth-ounce pink jigs. Within three hours they had hooked 14 steelhead. The other 12 anglers hadn't taken any. I believed Nick's story, but assumed it was a freak accident. I didn't even consider rushing out to buy some jigs.

Then another friend called to tell me of a day of steelheading on the Wilson River. He had hired a top guide who had fruitlessly pulled plugs most of the day without a strike. My friend finally asked the guide if it would be okay to try some jigs. The guide was skeptical, almost hostile, but my friend persevered. By days end, my friend, who had been casting jigs, while the guide continued to pull plugs, had three steelhead. The plugs hadn't taken any. That story convinced me to buy a few jigs, which I carried but didn't fish for over a year.

My conversion came on the Wenatchee River on a golden fall day. I had been working a pool that I knew held fish—it always had before, and I had seen two fish roll near the tailout. I literally tossed everything in my vest at them—spinners, spoons, artificial eggs and egg clusters, even my trusty pink worm. Nothing. Finally, with more hope than expectation, I tied a pink and white one-quarter-ounce jig beneath a small float. On my second cast the float was yanked under. I set the hook, too hard, and broke off a fine, red-cheek steelhead. With shaking hands I tied on my only other jig, a chartreuse and black one-quarter-ounce model. Three casts later, I hooked my second steelhead on a jig. By now, of course, I was hooked as well.

Drew and I and many of our friends are convinced that on many occasions jigs are a deadly tool for the serious salmon and steelhead angler. Unfortunately, many anglers haven't learned to use jigs, and many others who do use them are unaware of some of the tricks and tactics that can increase their success. We bring you this book in the same spirit as the 10-year-old who excitedly calls his friends to tell them how well red worms work for bluegill. Or the 70-year-old who shows a new fly to his angling club. We are excited about what we have discovered, and we want to share our find with you. We hope *Steelhead Jig Fishing* will bring you more angling pleasure by increasing your success with river salmon and steelhead.

The History of Steelheading with Jigs

Dave Vedder

Jigs are among the oldest forms of artificial lures known to man. Depending upon how loosely we define the term "jig," one can argue that the jig may have been the first artificial lure. If we define a jig as simply a weight with an attached attractor, jigs can be traced to the earliest days of sports fishing. There is ample evidence that jigs were very popular in the U.S. as far back as the early 1900s. My revered old copy of *Outdoor Life's* "Sportsman's Cyclopedia" circa 1942, advises that jigs are deadly for walleye, trout, bass and many panfish. They failed to mention steelhead, perhaps because no one had yet tried tempting steelhead with a jig.

The advent of jig fishing for steelhead in the Northwest can be traced to a fateful day in 1977, on the Cowlitz River. Steelheading fanatic Leo Gwazacz was having one of those days we all experience now and then—he couldn't buy a strike. In frustration, he began digging through his tackle box to see if he could find something, anything, that might prompt a strike.

An assortment of homemade floats from the collection of George Friskey.

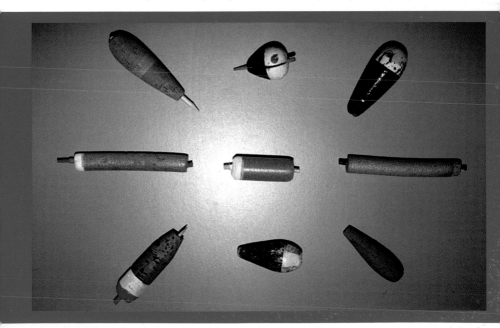

What he found was a small red-headed, lead jig wrapped with white chenille. He thought it looked like something a steelhead might pick-up, so he gave it a try. Three casts later, Northwest steelheading was forever changed. A Cowlitz River steelhead proved to Leo what thousands of other steelheaders were eventually to learn; many times and in many places nothing will outfish a properly-presented jig.

At first, Leo wasn't certain whether he had discovered a hot new lure, or if he had just found one kamikaze steelhead. Leo began fishing jigs regularly, and he began taking steelhead regularly. He soon realized that he was onto something big. Leo soon began making his own jigs, experimenting with various color combinations of chenille body wrap. Eventually, he began sharing his jigs with friends. Within a few years, Leo's success with jigs became well known among Northwest steelhead fanatics. Leo couldn't keep up with demand. He began mass manufacturing, and marketed "Leo's Jigs."

In the next few years Leo and his son, Leo, Junior, made many changes in the design of their jigs. Leo, Junior is credited with the idea of adding colored beads to the hook shank for added attraction. Leo, Senior believes the beads remind steelhead of the shape and silhouette of a shrimp. Whatever the steelhead may think, they certainly go for jigs with bead bodies. Today, Leo's Jigs are among the best selling steelhead jigs in the Northwest.

Paul Beaupre was another pioneer in the Northwest steelhead jig fishing industry. Paul began manufacturing and selling a line of innovative steelhead and salmon lures

An assortment of Beau Mac Jigs.

in 1982. In the early 1980s one of Paul's favorite lures was the Pearl Head Shrimp, an artificial lure featuring a bead head and a chenille body. It was a dynamite steelhead lure. Paul saw Leo's Jigs featured a lead head and a bead body and decided to add a bit of lead to the head of his Pearl Head Shrimp. The result was the forerunner of the tremendously popular Big Jig and Jig-A-Lou, the latter being named after his wife, Mary Lou. Both lures, invented independently by innovative anglers, combined colorful beads on the hook shank, bright colors and a lead head jig. Approaching the issue from different perspectives these two men developed jigs that are still among the best in the West.

No discussion of jig fishing history would be complete without acknowledging the tremendous contributions of Jim Bradbury. Jim has spent years perfecting his marabou jigs and teaching steelheaders how to fish them.

Great Lakes area steelhead and salmon anglers rely on jigs more with each passing year. Many of the region's top anglers use almost nothing else. The strong preference shown for jigs by Midwest anglers has resulted in a proliferation of jigs of every possible size, shape and color. Great Lakes jig anglers have a choice of more than fifty factory designs and as many homemade varieties as the imagination will allow. Given the huge popularity of jigs in the Great Lakes region, tracing the evolution of jig fishing to its roots has proven almost impossible. But most Great Lakes anglers agree Gill Rice was a pioneer who popularized the use of jigs for steelhead.

Gill's story is much like that of Leo Gwazacz on the west coast, except Gill experienced his revelation at least five years sooner than Leo. Gill, who has for years guided for steelhead on the Muskegon River, had taken a break from steelheading to catch a few yellow perch for dinner. He was using a locally popular perch jig called a "tear drop" in the one-eighth-ounce size. Gill fished the small red jig tipped with a grub. To his surprise, he found he was consistently hooking steelhead on his "perch jig."

Like any dedicated steelheader, Gill immediately did two things; he kept his discovery a secret and he began tinkering with his jigs to find ways to make them more effective. For several years Gill was able to keep his secret. Then one day another angler "accidentally" cast across Gill's line and got a good look at the secret weapon while untangling the lines. The secret was out. Soon many anglers on the Muskegon and White rivers were steelheading with jigs. Today, many of the region's top rods consider jigs the most deadly possible steelhead lure. Most Great Lakes anglers combine the visual appeal of jigs with the alluring scent of spawn sacks, grubs or other favorite steelhead baits.

The Advantages of Fishing with Jigs

Drew Harthorn

There are advantages and disadvantages to fishing with just one method for steelhead. The steelhead jig is no different. Over the years I've discovered that the method of suspending a jig under a float carries one huge disadvantage: Most dyed-in-the-wool steelheaders don't consider it "real" steelheading. Matter of fact, most of them won't fish with anything but eggs and yarn. This leaves jig and float anglers feeling inferior—like we're a pack of morons. Floats, or bobbers as they used to be referred to, are commonly associated with trout fishing in a lake. And that's where the disadvantages end.

The advantages of fishing a jig suspended under a float far outnumber the disadvantages. With the jig riding at least eighteen inches off the bottom, hang-ups are rare compared to the traditional drift gear method. This alone is a huge advantage. Applying the politician's economic trickle-down theory to jig fishing opens up a lot of other benefits. It's like money in the bank. I find this tool (lures are tools, aren't they?), extremely helpful for beginning steelhead anglers. I often fish my clients with jigs. When they're taking a guided steelhead trip, they like to have a hands-on experience. Instead of just sitting there watching plug rods, they're casting and learning to read water. Learning how and where to cast is half the battle of steelheading. Floats let you see the way river currents move your gear in the river. In the event that you want to use drift gear, your experience with floats will give you a much better understanding of what's going on down there.

Having coached a number of young anglers, I know that keeping their bait in the water is a good way to keep them occupied. With jigs they have very few hang-ups, which keeps them fishing, and it also allows everyone else in the fishing party to keep a lure wet.

For new anglers, picking up the subtle bite of a steelhead on traditional gear can be frustrating. With a jig and float, there's little doubt when a steelhead has taken the jig—the float is simply pulled under. That's the advantage. The disadvantage is that you have to keep at least one eye trained on the float because the strike is primarily visual. (Eventually you will find that you feel many strikes as soon as, or sooner than, you see them.)

Suspended jigs can be fished in various water conditions like: Normal drift water, slow water, fast water, against a rock wall or clay bank, and

A sample of the wide variety of jigs available to today's steelheader.

over suspended fish. Casting a jig against a clay bank or rock ledge has become one of my most deadly presentations. Traditional drift gear will swing in an arc away from the wall, even when the bait is free-spooled trying to increase the drift length.

The float will drift as close to the clay bank as you wish, depending on where you placed the cast. And it will maintain the same line of drift for as long as you wish.

Time after time fish have been hooked in this kind of area even after traditional drift gear has passed through the hole. Deep water associated with clay banks and rock ledges also hold suspended fish. Fishing on the bottom with traditional gear will put the offering well below the fish's range of vision. Suspending a jig above them gives you a chance to hook one. The same thing goes for a textbook steelhead run.

Success with jigs almost goes hand-in-hand with water color and clarity. You're at a real disadvantage fishing a jig in off-color or stained water. I feel if there's at least four feet of visibility, you will have a good chance of success. Less than that, you're simply wearing out the ball bearings in your reel. When the water is low and clear—a steelheader's nightmare—jigs really step up to the plate and deliver. If you use a neutral colored jig in such water, white or light pink, fish that normally would spook will climb on a jig.

In clear water the jig can be fished as much as three or four feet off the bottom if there's sufficient water depth. This is a big advantage because the

Clint Derlago works his way to a fishy-looking pocket in a fast water run. These are not high percentage areas, but they are worth a few casts.

jig is visible to more fish. There have been times when all I've seen is the huge flash of a mint-bright steelhead and the instantaneous disappearance of the float. That means only one thing—you fooled another one.

Fishing a jig in fast water is about the least effective method, but it can be done. Rolling and boiling white water is the hardest to fish, but it's often water that's passed up by drift-gear anglers. Even though this type of water is low percentage water, once in a while you might get surprised.

Being able to fish a slow-moving drift that's littered with basketball size boulders and not hang up is another big plus for jig fishing. I admit it. I throw a lot of drift gear and bait, but when it comes to boulder gardens, the jig is the only way to go. About the time you think about casting that pencil lead and drift bobber combination into a boulder garden, you're thinking that it's a sure-death cast. If there isn't a fish laying behind the rock that you just cast to, the next rock downstream will gobble your lead, drift bobber and bait so fast, you won't even know what happened. But a suspended jig will float right by.

No matter what type of water you fish, a suspended jig will move at the same speed as the current. It's a very natural presentation. And the more natural your presentation, the more hook-ups you'll have.

Basics of Jig Fishing

Drew Harthorn

Steelhead fishing doesn't have to be technical. Fishing with a jig is far from it. In fact, it's downright easy. One of the hardest things for a seasoned steelhead angler to conquer is the stigma that fishing with a float is for. . .crackers. Cracker is a term widely used by steelheaders referring to someone not well versed at steelhead fishing. But fishing a jig under a float can be extremely effective at times. And that's when the savvy, sometimes cunning, steelhead angler ties on a jig and float.

Through the years of fishing with a jig and float, I've seen many refinements take place with the tackle and technique. In the early days, it wasn't uncommon to hook a fish and then lose it. The hook would either straighten out, or the fish would simply come off. To combat the problem of losing fish, we started pinching down the barb and making sure the hook was sticky sharp. Because the roof of a steelhead's mouth is very bony, we were having trouble getting good penetration with our jig hooks. Once we began pinching the barbs and sharpening our hooks to razor points, we noticed that our jigs were usually impaled clear through in the tip of the steelhead's upper lip. That was full penetration. The percentage of landed fish skyrocketed.

Jig fishing is simple in comparison to other techniques. Besides the rod and reel, you only need a float, a jig, and a few split shot. Rigging a steelhead jig set up starts with the float. With all of the different styles of floats available, one of the most popular is the non-fixed, or sliding variety. This is where the main line can pass freely through the float. This type is a personal favorite. Little known to most anglers, this also becomes a "poor man's depth sounder." A sliding float is versatile in the sense that you can instantly adjust for the different depth of a run just by sliding the stopper up or down the line. If you choose to use a different style of float, pick one that allows you to read what the jig is doing. After selecting a float, all you need to do is tie on a jig.

Often times I am asked what my favorite color of jig is. I usually don't respond to that question with a direct answer, because I look at jigs in shades (light, medium and dark) versus colors. Limiting yourself to the use of one or two colors of a jig will . . . limit you. Steelhead anglers can be very superstitious about the colors of tackle they fish. Some say red, others say peach. Others favor orange, white, black or purple. And then there's my co-author who swears by Beau Mac's pink Marabou Jig. It's endless.

That's why I recommend shades.

When the lighting is low, in the early morning or late evening, or the water color is stained, a lighter/brighter shade of jig works well. In normal water conditions, medium shades should be used. When the water is clear, and the sun is bright, a dark or light shade should be used. Don't take this as gospel because there are many situations when the fish will take what they want to. If you spot fish or know there are fish in a particular run and they don't take your offering, switch colors. The choice of color I'm leaving up to you. It's a confidence thing. If you think you're going to catch a steelhead with a particular color, then fish that color.

Jigs that are suspended under a float can be fished where standard steelhead gear can't. The three most popular drifts to fish jigs in are boulder patches, along steep clay or rock banks, and slow water. Tossing typical drift gear into a boulder patch can result in many hang ups and retying of terminal tackle. Suspended jigs glide through and around boulders and rocks with ease. Fished along a clay bank or rock wall, the float will magically hug the wall precisely where steelhead like to lay. They also drift along in slow water where pencil lead will stop the drift. But this isn't the only type of water you can fish a jig in. You can fish in standard runs as well as fast water.

Floating a jig in what I consider less that desirable water for drift gear anglers, opens up some unfished water for the jig angler. With increased competition for decreasing runs of steelhead, anglers must look for unfished water.

The idea behind suspending a jig under a float is to present a bait at a

Early morning low light con-
ditions and a fast moving tai-
lout are often the combina-
tion for success.

natural pace and depth for the steelhead to see. Contrary to popular belief, not all steelhead lay on the bottom of the river. Some fish either suspend and hold in one spot, or get up off the bottom and head upriver. Drift gear anglers target the fish that lay and hold on or near the bottom of the river, often times passing up suspended fish. Most of the time, unknowingly.

To properly fish a suspended jig, the jig should precede the float downriver. The best way to determine this is by reading the stem of the float. If the stem is leaning slightly backwards (upriver), it means the jig is trying to pull the float downriver. That is exactly the way it is supposed to be. On the other hand, if the stem of the float is pointed downriver, it means the jig is being pulled downriver. That's not what you want.

Jigs used for steelheading are similar to crappie or bass jigs. They are generally made on either 1/0 or 2/0 hooks with a lead head weighing one-sixteenth to one-fourth ounce. By design, if a lead head jig is pulled through the water, the lead head will come first, followed by the lighter, hook end or tail of the jig. The point here is: You want the business end of the hook to enter the fish's mouth first, not the lead head. In order for that to happen, the float has to create some upriver pull on the jig. In essence, it's like you're pulling the jig upriver. That is why the stem of the float must be pointed slightly upriver.

Getting the stem to ride just right can be a hassle. Stem angle can vary from drift to drift depending on the speed of the current and depth of the run. One of the best ways to correct stem angle is to add a small split shot

Basics of Jig Fishing

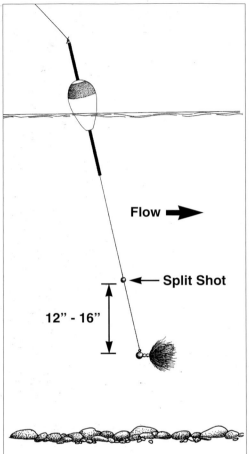

Your float should be tilted slightly upstream. This indicates that you are holding back ever so slightly and tells you that your jig is floating above the bottom.

to the line approximately twelve inches above the jig but below the float. If you're worried that the split shot might damage your line, an alternative would be to slide a small piece of surgical tubing on the line and add a small piece of pencil lead. The amount of lead is a hit-and-miss proposition. You'll have to experiment to find a happy medium.

In optimum river conditions, the jig should be fished 18 to 24 inches off the bottom. If water conditions allow (clear water), the distance from the bottom can be increased to 36 inches. Since steelhead can't see down worth a darn, anything floating above them is a candidate to be munched. I'm not exactly sure what steelhead think one of these jigs represents, but their curiosity sure makes jig fishing fun.

I'm often asked if you need to put some kind of scent on the jig. Jig fishing is primarily a sight thing. If the jig you're putting in the water is stinky, chances are it won't get bit. Clean jigs, with a drop of scent surely can't hurt. I prefer the Dr. Juice Steelhead scent, but that's not to say others won't work. Bottom line: When a fish sees the jig and likes what it sees, they flat out jump all over it. If you are accustomed to using scent, go ahead and use it. One tip though: Make sure you completely clean the jig after your day of fishing. Scents have a way of drying and gumming up the jig. Ultimately, it destroys the action of the jig.

Another important factor in steelhead jig fishing is maintaining a tight line to the float. This can be enhanced by using a long rod. Either style of

rod, spinning or bait casting, at least 10 feet long will suffice. Canadian steelhead anglers often use rods measuring 13 feet or longer. The main idea is to keep the belly in the line to a minimum. The tighter the line, the greater chance there is to get a solid hook up. To assist in keeping the line mended, as fly anglers do, and running straight to the float, I suggest coating the first 75 feet of the line with paraffin wax, fly floatant or mucilin. As the float drifts down the river, wax-coated monofilament line lifts easily off the water, allowing you to make a tight line hook set.

One of the beauties of fishing a float is the length of the drift. Unlike drift fishing, floats allow you to cover more water. This might peeve drift gear anglers, especially if there are a couple of them standing next to you. Drift and float fishing are not very compatible. In the interest of being a good sportsman, keep your drifts about the same length as the anglers fishing around you. If you're in a secluded area, or have the run to yourself, feel free to extend your drift. This is best controlled by using a bait casting or centerpin reel combination, leaving it in free-spool, and thumbing or palming the spool, slowly letting line out while keeping a tight line. Often a fish will pull the jig under at the very end of the sweep, just like a spoon or spinner.

Knowing when a fish bites on a suspended jig is no mystery. The most common bite or takedown is having the float disappear under the water. There are only two things that cause this to happen: a fish is pulling on your jig, or the jig has hung up on something. In either case, you need to

Ed Larm, manufacturer of
Mr. Ed's Floats, shows how
well a float and jig combo
can work. This two-salt
hatchery fish fell for a
Nightmare Jig fished
beneath a Mr. Ed's Float.

An assortment of floats
appropriate for fishing with
small jigs.

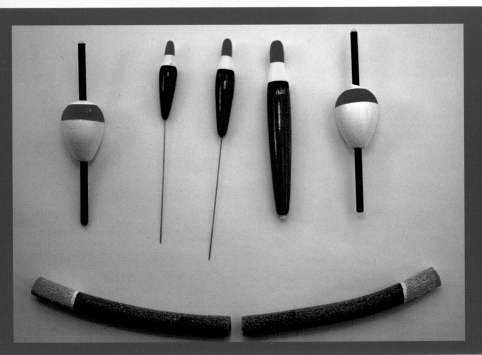

Jig Fishing for Steelhead

smartly set the hook. You don't need to give it one of those Roland Martin big bass hook sets, but you really need to sting them.

Having the float rapidly disappear isn't the only type of bite you might encounter. Occasionally, the float will simply stop and move to one side or the other. In this case, it's necessary to watch the float to see if it's a fish. If it moves a substantial amount, set the hook. This is all fine and dandy in a typical steelhead run where the water is fairly smooth, but fast water is a little different.

Jigs are the least productive in boiling white water. This is not to say that fish haven't been caught in this type of water, but it's not my first target. The problem with fishing fast water is getting the jig down fast enough to make it into the fish zone. Adding split shot above the jig can help improve your chances.

Still waters are best fished with light lines, small floats and lures that provide a strong visual stimuli without the benefit of movement provided by strong current flows. Light lines are necessary because clear water and slow moving lures give steelhead ample opportunity to examine your offering.

Small floats are used because there is no need for the buoyancy required to keep the float visible in choppy water. Another reason for small floats is their increased sensitivity. Still water steelhead often nibble so delicately the bite is barely discernible. Tiny floats will telegraph these tiny bites.

Tackle for Jig Fishing

Dave Vedder

Successful jig fishing requires more than simply tying a jig onto the end of your line. To get the most from jig fishing you need to add at least two items to your arsenal—a float and a long rod. Jigs fish best under a float, floats work best with long rods. Those are two truths that must be considered before seriously considering adding jigs to your river fishing arsenal.

Rods for Jig Fishing

No other element of your jig fishing tackle is as important as your rod. Success with jig fishing demands that you make accurate casts to distant lies and do so with as much as 10 feet of line beneath your float. This dictates a rod of at least 10 and one half feet in length. To those who have never fished with a jig, this may seem like a ridiculous rod length. Those who have fished floats and jigs for years usually own several rods in the 12 to 15 foot range.

Clancy Holt shows a fine Cowlitz River steelhead taken with the G. Loomis 1141 spinning rod he designed.

The reasons for long rods are several. Perhaps the most important reason to use such a long rod is the need to keep your jig near the bottom of deep runs. Consider what happens when you try to fish a 12-foot-deep lie with a float using a standard 9-foot steelhead rod. You must slide your float up the line until you have something in the range of 10 feet or more of line between the float and the jig. Now you find that your 9-foot rod is too short to keep your jig off the ground. If your line is dragging in the dirt before you begin your cast, disaster awaits you.

Now let's say you have somehow managed to cast your float and its payload to that fishy looking seam on the far side of the run with your 9-foot rod. Even if you stand on a rock and hold your hands above your head, you can't keep the line off the water. As the currents tug at the line laying on the water, a belly will form in the line. Soon the line will be pulling the float to the side or pulling it downstream at an unnatural pace.

If you did happen to get your jig to the run you wanted to fish, and if you did manage to draw a strike, your short rod would still be your undoing. Because the rod is too short to keep your line off the water, you cannot avoid a significant amount of slack between your rod tip and the float. When the float goes down, you haul back mightily on the rod only to yank a few feet of slack line toward you. The float hasn't moved and the fish is now gone.

There is no way to avoid it. You are going to have to buy a 10 and one half foot rod. Later when you are fully hooked on jigs and floats, you may want to try even longer rods, but the 10 and one half foot rod is a fine all-purpose float and jig rod.

A few years ago, such rods were hard to find in the U.S. Fortunately several U.S. manufacturers make a fine selection of float rods. G. Loomis has a great selection and the finest float rods on the market. Their only drawback is a stiff price. Lamiglas now offers a fine selection of excellent rods at a reasonable price.

An all-purpose jig rod should have a strong backbone and still have enough sensitivity to telegraph strikes. Even though your float can act as a huge strike indicator, you will find that you can often feel the take as well as see it. An ideal float rod should be rated for 10 to 20 pound test line. It should weigh no more than eight and one half ounces. The handle length from the center of the reel seat to the butt plate should be more than 14 inches to give you the leverage for long casts. Those of you who use centerpin reels will need to select rods with longer foregrips and shorter handles.

Reels

Jig fishing places no special demands on a reel. Any reel you might use for fishing other lures should work well. There are however some jig fishing situations that dictate specific types of reels.

When fishing typical river lies where the water is moving briskly and the clarity is less than crystal clear, bait casting reels are the choice of most anglers. When fishing light tackle in clear water for spooky fish, a spinning reel is the best choice. A deadly low water combination is a small float with little or no weight between the float and a small jig. If the fish are very spooky, a six pound test main line, a small float, four pound test leader and a small jig is a deadly combination. Unfortunately, most bait casting and centerpin reels will not cast such light weight terminal gear. A spinning reel will, but at a price.

The spinning reel will deliver a lighter package than any other reel but it is a poor choice for drifting floats to downstream positions. To free-spool with a spinning reel, the bail must be in the open position. When the bail is open, it is hard to make a fast, solid hook set. For an open bail hook set you have two choices. You can trap the line between your fingers and the foregrip before setting the hook, or you can take the time to crank the reel handle to flip the bail back closed. Both methods have drawbacks. Trapping the line beneath your fingers may prove to be difficult if you are wearing gloves, or if your fingers are cold. Flipping the bail takes precious time, and unless you have the drag set very tight, you may still not get a solid hook set. If you choose to keep your drag tight to assure a solid hook set, you will need to act fast to loosen the drag as soon as you have a good hookup.

In spite of all its drawbacks, a long light rod rigged with a spinning reel is the optimum set up for low water, spooky steelhead. Like democracy, it's far from perfect, but it's the best we have.

Centerpin Reels

The centerpin reel is by far the favorite reel of the serious British Columbia and Great Lakes steelheader. This may be because it casts more smoothly than other reels, or because the direct drive reels require more skill on the angler's part than does a reel with gears. Or it simply may be a badge of competency that announces that this angler is a serious steelheader.

The centerpin reel is a bundle of good and bad that can only be judged by each of us individually. On the plus side of the ledger, these reels are extraordinarily smooth casting. They are usually quite nicely finished, and they allow you to free-spool your float with almost no drag. On the negative side, they can be the devil to learn to cast. The lack of gears makes it difficult to catch up to a fish that is running toward you and, likewise, they retrieve line more slowly than a typical reel with gears. This can cost a steelheader a good deal of time during a full day's angling. In addition, they are usually expensive. Still there's nothing quite the same as palming a single action reel while a big steelhead races downstream, then reeling frantically to catch up when the fish reverses course. If you think you are a real pro with a levelwind reel, give the centerpin a try. At first it will humble then it will thrill you.

Floats

Almost every jig fishing situation calls for a float. But there is far more to successfully working a jig than simply attaching your jig beneath a red and white plastic bobber. To fish jigs most effectively, you must have a balanced system of rod, reel, float, weights and terminal tackle, all selected to work in harmony.

There is no one best float for jig fishing just as there is no one best rod, reel, or jig. Selecting the proper float requires that you give consideration to the type of water you will be fishing, and the combined weight of the jig and lead you intend to fish.

Two of the best steelhead floats are the simple foam floats widely used in British Columbia, known as "dink" floats, and the balsa floats commonly used in the Great Lakes region and now rapidly gaining popularity in the Northwest. Both share the attributes of being infinitely and rapidly adjustable, and both come in a sufficient variety of sizes and shapes to suit almost any steelheading situation.

The dink float is inexpensive and can easily be modified to suit almost any water condition. Most dink floats are four to six inches in length, approximately one half inch in diameter and feature a brightly painted top

Today's float anglers have a large variety of floats to choose from. Always try to use the smallest float that will adequately carry the weight and jig you wish to fish.

for ease of visibility. Favorite colors are red, orange and chartreuse. Orange and red are most easily seen in low light conditions, and chartreuse is best in the middle of the day.

Most dink floats are threaded onto the line via a center tunnel or angled tubes at each end of the float. Center tunnel tubes are held in place either by a toothpick or a thin bamboo reed that comes with the float. Floats with angled tubes at top and bottom rely on a wrap of line around the float to create sufficient friction to hold the float in place.

Mr Ed's Floats, manufactured in Camas, Washington, come in several sizes that work quite well with jigs. The N.A.S. float designed by Nick Amato, is small enough to work slow clear water with light weight and small jigs, yet the total weight of float and terminal gear is sufficient to cast well with a bait casting reel. On the other end of the scale his V.V. (Vedder's Vengeance) float will carry as much as two ounces of weight which makes it ideal for fishing big water where long casts are required.

Among the dink floats I prefer the dense foam models over the lighter and softer versions. The dense foam floats carry more weight and last longer than soft foam floats.

Balsa floats are the most lovely of the floats and many prefer the buoyancy of balsa over foam. They are a pleasure to fish, and they are often beautifully finished. Balsa floats come in a variety of sizes ranging from

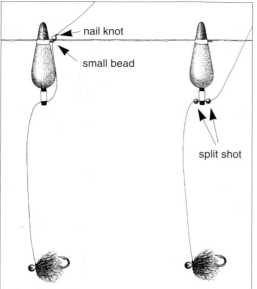

nail knot

small bead

split shot

Many balsa floats can be rigged both as a slip float and as fixed floats depending upon how you wish to fish them.

the dime sized Thill River Master to the six inch Big Fish Slider. Many balsa floats are designed to be quickly interchangeable, and most are held to the line by silicone sleeves that can quickly be removed to change floats. The top of most balsa floats are painted with two bands of bright color. The top band marks the ideal water level for fishing quiet waters. The bottom of the yellow band marks the proper float height for fast water.

Weighting your Float

There are as many ways to weight a float system as the imagination allows, but all have these important attributes: The float must be weighted so that it protrudes only slightly above the water and the jig must work its magic near the river bottom. How those attributes are achieved is less important than assuring that these two imperatives are met.

The weights used to properly balance a float are usually split shot ranging in size from the largest magnum shot to fine dust. Shot are ideal weights as they can be added and deleted as needed until the float sits properly in the water. In recent years many float anglers have experimented with small eared sinkers that have the added benefits of rapid removal and that they may be reused repeatedly. The rubber cored removable sinkers also work well. If you carry three sizes, you can quickly

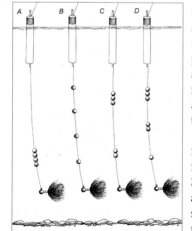

Several weighting systems can be employed to properly weight your jig and float. Your choice depends on water clarity and current speed. In slow, clear water use a system that keeps the weights as unobtrusive as possible.

adjust to almost any water condition.

When weighting your float with multiple weights, it is important that you space the weight correctly to avoid tangles. A single group of weights work well as do several equally spaced weights. Two weights separated by a foot or more of monofilament, with a jig a few feet beneath, form an unstable aerodynamic which almost guarantees tangles.

Other weighting systems including pencil lead, slinkys and hollow core lead. All have proven to be satisfactory. My favorite system is an in-line slinky. I simply attach a snap swivel to each end of a slinky and tie my main line to one swivel and the leader to the other. This system seldom hangs up and I can change slinkys rapidly by simply unsnapping two swivels.

Leaders

Leaders used beneath floats run the gamut from 20 pound test to one pound test and from 14 inches long to eight feet long. In the big colored waters of Western rivers, short heavy leaders work well and are often necessary to land big fish in fast water. In the more gentle waters of Great Lakes rivers, it is usually necessary to go to long, light leaders to draw a strike.

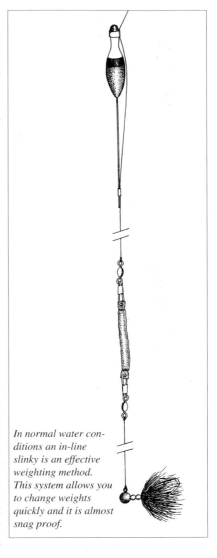

In normal water conditions an in-line slinky is an effective weighting method. This system allows you to change weights quickly and it is almost snag proof.

Leaders should be attached to the main line with a swivel. Top quality ball bearing swivels will eliminate line twist that can be a problem. Ultra light leaders of three pound test or less are commonly attached directly to the main line without a swivel. Abrasion resistant, non visible material is usually best for leaders. Ande Tournament and Berkley XT are excellent choices. When fishing with long, light leaders, Berkley XL and others specially formulated for limpness are ideal.

Choosing the Right Jig

Drew Harthorn

Choosing the correct jig is just as important as having fish in the river. Depending on water conditions, hook size, jig size, and the color of the jig will vary. A lot of the steelhead jigs on the market are made using a traditional crappie jig style of hook. In order to hold on to a big steelhead many tackle manufacturers have opted to use bigger and stronger hooks. Most all of the jigs manufactured use a lead head with either colored yarn or marabou feathers for the body. Jigs vary by manufacturer. Some directly tie the marabou feathers to the shank of the hook while others place a series of beads on the hook and slide in colored yarn. Either style of jig will fish fine.

Low, slow, and clear river conditions dictate using a jig that's small and subtle. This is especially true in late August when the rivers are low and clear. The same principle applies when the rivers are low, cold and clear in the winter. Subtle is the key.

In terms of shades versus colors, a light or dark jig will work as well for low, clear water. A favorite color among steelheaders is white. A combination of white and pink also works well, as does peach or a combination of white and peach. Loud colors are an absolute no-no. When fishing low, clear water Black and purple also work well. One of my favorite colors is blue.

Size of the jig is just as important as the color choice. For clear conditions, a small jig is in order. I normally don't use anything larger than a 1/0 hook with a 1/16-ounce lead head. Subdued colors and small jigs lend themselves to the stealthy approach so often employed by savvy steelhead anglers.

For "normal" conditions, if there really is such a thing, the size and color spectrum is almost wide open. Light shades work fine, but this is where the medium shades really kick in. This angler considers pink a crossover shade that fishes well in normal conditions. Blue also fits this category. Hook size can vary from 1/0 to 3/0 and lead heads weighing up to 1/4-ounce are common.

If you are, or happen to become, a die-hard jig angler and have to fish in less than ideal conditions (stained or colored water), big and bright becomes the key. Chartreuse, flame, red, and fluorescent orange are the colors of choice. In addition, Beau Mac Enterprises has come up with a line of jigs that are glow-in-the-dark. Not only does the tail of the jig glow after you flash it with a light source, but the painted lead head does too. This jig has also proven to be deadly on steelhead while night fishing at spots like Blue Creek on Washington's Cowlitz River.

One of the questions I get asked most is "what is your favorite color

These beautiful jigs by John Koenig, feature rabbit fur bodies that drive steelhead crazy.

jig?" I usually respond with blue, followed by white. I like blue. Blue fits a neutral category that I really haven't mentioned. For clear conditions, it's very subdued. Not too flashy. For normal conditions, it absorbs enough light to be visible to the fish. In adverse river conditions, blue is dark enough to give off an adequate silhouette. What else would you want?

So what about white? White works well in clear and normal conditions. At times, nothing works as well as white, and that's when you'll find a white jig hanging off the end of this angler's rod. The most important thing here though is to use what you have confidence in. If you feel good about pink, or a mixed pink/white jig, then use that. Confidence in what you're using is bigger than you think.

I picked up on something a guide friend, Ron Rodgers, said once, it went something like this: Always let the fish tell you what they want. Don't tell them. If you only fish white jigs and the crowd around you is slamming' fish on pink jigs, you better be putting on a pink jig. On the other hand, if the crowd all have pink jigs on and nobody is hitting fish, I'd surely tie something on other than pink. Experiment until you find something that works.

Obtaining the ultimate blend between river conditions and sunlight (or lack of it) is the ultimate challenge for jig anglers. To get started, you need at least six basic jigs: two from each of the shade categories: light, medium and dark. From the light category, try a pink and a white. From the medium group, take a red and an orange. For dark jigs, I'd suggest black and, of course, blue. If you have a strong feeling for other colors, have them on hand.

Jigs are fairly inexpensive. They cost more than traditional drift bobbers, but less than a top of the line spinner. We all like to save on costs when fishing. The cheaper you can do it, the better off you are.

On the Water

Drew Harthorn

One of the most important things to remember when approaching a river or stream is to do it quietly. Having the killer jig tied on the end of your line won't do a damn thing for you if you spook the fish. When conditions permit, such as cloudy water, approaching the river in a stealthy manner isn't quite as important.

Steelhead tend to stack low in the hole early in the morning. The tailout is a prime area to start working. Often times, if the water is clear enough, spotting fish is easy with the aid of polarized glasses. There's nothing as exciting as approaching the stream bank, spotting a few fish holding

Clint Derlago casts across a golden pool in a Vancouver Island stream.

in the tailout, and anticipating a hook up on the first cast.

This situation warrants going for the icing on the cake versus starting your meal with a salad. Most of the time, I suggest methodically cutting the river into little pieces—probing every square foot. But when fish are visible, go for them. A jig suspended under a float is a very natural-paced presentation, more so than traditional drift gear. Steelhead laying in the tailout are looking for the easy meal. Tempting them with a jig is a quick way to provide yourself some entertainment.

This all sounds very simple, but if it was so easy, everybody out there would be catching lots of steelhead. Here's the formula that works for me: Set the slip float so there's about two-feet of line to the jig. Lightly pinch a single 1/16-ounce split shot about 12 inches above the jig on the main line, and cast directly above the fish. The cast should be made far enough upstream from the fish to allow the jig plenty of time to settle before it reaches the fish. By that, I mean that the jig has pulled down all the line between the jig and the slip float, and the stem of the float is riding vertically against the line stopper.

Once the jig has settled, the excess line will have to be taken in. It can be as simple as reeling in the slack, but that might change the line the jig is running. If you need to pick up slack, but want to leave the jig on its current course, you'll have to perform something fly anglers refer to as "mending the line." Mending monofilament line is like trying to pry a sticky spaghetti noodle off the kitchen ceiling. A little trick here is to wax the first 75 feet of your line with paraffin wax or mucilin. You'll find that monofilament line now slides right off the water and can be easily mended (lifted upstream). Water will roll off the line like water on a duck's back.

Back to the fish. As the jig and float make their way downstream, it's important to keep a fairly tight line. When a steelhead takes the jig, the float will dip under the surface and disappear. Now it's time to set the hook. That's how it normally happens. In the event that there was some slack line bellied out in the current, a good solid hook set might not take place. A long rod in the 10 to 12-foot range will help combat a weak hook set because it helps pull more line off the water than a rod that's between eight to nine feet long. This is not to say though that a nine-foot-long rod couldn't be used. But a short rod will lower your percentage of solid hook sets.

Jig fishing in clear water offers a lot of surprises in comparison to "regular water." Steelhead can see great distances when the conditions are right. So when you are casting to visible fish, expect the unexpected: A fish coming out of nowhere. There have been a few times I've been caught off-guard casting to visible fish. That "fish from nowhere" has creamed the jig on a couple of occasions and startled me so bad that I didn't get a good hook set and ultimately lost the fish.

As the sunlight starts to appear in the morning, steelhead like to reposition themselves further up in the hole where there might be some cover. One of the beauties of fishing a sliding float is that it's instantly adjustable. To make a depth change, only the stop has to be moved up the main line. If you suspect there's six feet of water, slide the stop so there's four feet of line out. If you end up moving to the head of the hole where there's 10 feet of water, move the line stop so there's eight feet of line out. It's that simple. The traditional red/white, round, plastic bobber just doesn't cut it. In a pinch though, it is better than nothing.

Float adjustment is so easy with a sliding float it makes fishing an entire drift a snap. In the earlier scenario with fish stacked in the tailout, a short line was necessary since most tailouts are almost always shallow. As you move up the hole into deeper water, the depth of the jig can be easily adjusted. The point here is that jigs can be fished in a normal steelhead run quite effectively with minimal hassle.

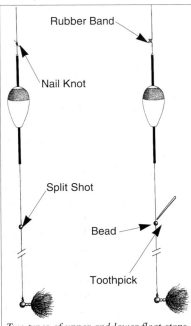

Two types of upper and lower float stops. On the left the upper stop employs a nail knot and a bead. The lower stop is simply a small split shot. The illustration on the right shows a knotted rubber band for an upper stop and small bead and toothpick for a lower stop. Top and bottom stops keep your jig working even when holding back.

When river conditions are in a "normal" winter status as far as color, clarity, and height, I like to start fishing a drift at the head of the hole and work my way downstream. It's essentially the same as traditional drift fishing. In a typical steelhead run, jigs are fished much like conventional drift gear. The only thing you might have to adjust for is the depth of water. Adjusting the float is easy with the use of a line stopper. The line stopper can be fashioned out of several things besides the commercially available type.

The two commercial float stops you most often find in the tackle shops are the little pieces of plastic with three or four small holes punched in and small hollow tubes with nail knots tied to them. With the plastic float stops main line is threaded through the holes that provides enough friction to keep it in place. You can also use a small rubber band by folding it in half, looping it around the main line and drawing it back through itself. Trim the excess loop of

rubber band, and you have it. To use the nail knot as a float stop, all you need to do is slip your main line through the hollow tube and slide a pre-tied nail knot onto your line. Then tighten the nail knot onto your monofilament main line. The next step is to slip a small plastic bead onto your line below the nail knot. Then attach your float to the main line. Your float will slide up the line as far as you have positioned the nail knot. The nail knot stops the bead and the bead stops the float.

Another way to make a stopper is by using brightly colored steelhead yarn. Tie a couple of overhand knots and trim off the excess yarn, this creates a highly visible stopper. All three types of stoppers will easily pass through the eyes of most rods. This allows you to make casts in tight areas, such as overhanging brush and limbs. The only thing that is sticking out at the end of the rod is the amount of line from the float to the jig, which is usually 18 inches. Upon casting, you might feel a slight bumping as the stopper passes through the eyes. It's good practice to check the stopper every few casts to make sure it hasn't slipped from its set position.

One thing that's not thought about too much is the use of a lower stopper. This would be located below the float. For the most part, it isn't necessary to add a separate lower stopper because the split shot you've added between the float and jig to trim the stem angle acts as the lower stopper. The lower stopper serves a purpose, it keeps the jig in the water at the end of a drift.

The best way to relate this is by comparing it to a spoon or spinner. As a spoon or spinner swings around below you from the current pushing it, it

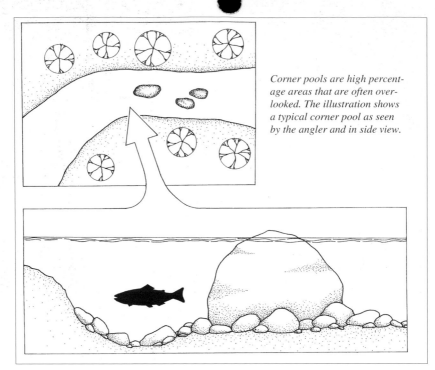

Corner pools are high percentage areas that are often overlooked. The illustration shows a typical corner pool as seen by the angler and in side view.

has a tendency to rise and eventually end up on the surface. The jig will do the same thing. A lower stopper will keep the jig in the water for that extra moment—that extra moment when a steelhead might take a jig. I don't want to overplay this aspect, but there have been many occasions when a steelhead thumped my jig just as I was going to start reeling in.

So, what about non-typical steelhead water? Some of that water most steelhead anglers pass up? When the river makes a bend, or an exposed gravel bar sticks out where it forms a shelf, I like to stick my jig there first. There are couple of reasons: It's nice holding water, and this type of water is seldom fished. This is not something I'd consider to be high percentage water, but good enough to make a few casts.

From this point, look for the area in the river where the slow water meets the fast water and forms a seam. In the saltchuck, salmon anglers call it a rip line. It's here that you'll often find the beginning of a ledge that runs parallel to the river bank. This is also a likely travel lane for the fish. I like to call these areas "steelhead freeways." So, just how do you know if you've found one of these freeways? An easy way to tell is where a flat or a gently sloped gravel bar suddenly drops off. More than likely, once it drops off, it will maintain some depth. This type of area is best spotted when there's low water. When the river raises back to a normal level, this should

Today's steelheaders have an enormous number of colors and combinations to choose from.

be one of your target areas. Many times you'll find steelhead anglers standing in the middle of them—right to the top of their boots and only a few feet from the river bank.

Oftentimes, you'll be able to cast your jig and float behind a deep wading angler and hook fish. I can only imagine how embarrassing this is for the angler that's standing in the river casting to the other side. Oh, I do know how that feels, but it only happened once. After sneaking your jig along the travel lane, start probing the river further out in five to six-foot increments. Quarter your cast upstream. Make full drifts with the jig and allow it to finish the drift by swinging straight down below you. Reel in, and make another cast five or six feet further out and repeat until that particular piece of water is covered.

To continue fishing out the drift, move down river to the approximate location that your jig was previously finishing its drift. Start with casting close in and, again, methodically work the river until the entire drift has been covered. So, what if you hit a fish? Stay there. Once you locate steelhead, there's a good chance you'll find more in the same general area. There's a reason for them being there. They like the speed of the current or that particular depth of the water. Depth and speed have a lot to do with locating steelhead. They're sensitive to these conditions. A fellow guide buddy of mine has spent a lot of time tracking these fish with a depth sounder/fish finder. He has found that holding areas and travel lanes stay rather consistent.

Now, seeing as how the average steelhead angler probably won't have a fish finder in his back pocket, the jig and float becomes a "poor man's depth sounder." To find out how deep a drift is, simply adjust the float until the jig contacts the bottom. You'll be able to tell this when the float is bouncing quite rapidly. At this point, you need to bring the jig and float in. Leaving this out too long might cause the jig to become a permanent fixture on the bottom.

Steelheaders are known to be secretive at times. Well, how about most of the time. Using the jig and float as a depth sounder has paid off on many occasions. As mentioned earlier, steelhead are sensitive to current. Sometimes, to avoid a strong current situation, they seek deeper water. But how do you know what that magical depth is? Luck? Hardly! If I've hit a fish, or have seen fish hooked, I'll discretely slide the jig and float through that area to find out how deep the drift is that these fish were taken in. Then I'll target that depth in other areas. Steelheading really is a game of inches: depth of water, length of cast, size of bait, etc.

On occasion, you'll run into an area that's not conducive to fishing in a normal mode with drift gear. For example: Throwing typical drift gear in a

Many inexperienced anglers pass up boulder gardens such as this. Steelhead hold throughout this type of water.

The best way to master jig fishing is with hands-on experience.

hole that's 15 or 20 feet deep with fish suspended a few feet from the surface will prove fruitless. A jig suspended only a few feet down that remains in the fish's cone of vision will increase the chance of a hook up.

Then there's the rock garden. This is an area littered with Yugo-sized boulders that you know is loaded with fish but would be a sure-death cast with pencil lead and bait. A suspended jig will float around boulders and sneak into those fish holding pockets, ultimately setting up another strength test on your monofilament line by a thrashing steelhead. This is the kind of water that makes me quiver when I spot it. Boulders make a natural resting spot for migrating steelhead. Knowing that most drift gear anglers will pass this type of water up, I jump right in there.

The first thing I do is plop the jig and float on the most likely-looking boulder out there. I let it slither down the side of the rock all the while bracing my feet from possibly slipping when I set the hook. As the jig swirls in the eddy behind the rock I know there's a good chance a steelhead will be looking at the jig. If nobody is home, cast to the next boulder. The one thing about pocket-pitching behind boulders is that I know right away if fish are there or not. Usually, if someone is home, it's an instant take.

I finish out the boulder garden by exploring all of the rocks, front and back. Sliding a jig in front of a boulder isn't as risky as you might think. Believe it or not, fish lay in front of big rocks as well as behind them. Fish all of the seams created by the current breaks around the boulders. If all of this fails, go find another drift. Be flexible.

As with any fishing method, presentation is a key element. A properly presented steelhead jig will keep pace with other techniques in the right conditions. I'd like to say that this book will give you all of the answers to jig fishing for steelhead, but I'd be lying. There are many variables that can't possibly be covered in a book. It comes down to hands-on experience. The best piece of advice I can give is to be flexible and multi-dimensional.

Don't get stuck on one thing. That can happen much too easily. With this new-found technique, it would be easy and convenient to only fish a float and jig, but you would be missing out on other opportunities. Just remember, every technique has its own time and place.

Still Water Jig Fishing

Dave Vedder

Many steelheaders never have the chance to fish steelhead in still water, but the opportunity does arise. Perhaps the most heavily fished steelhead water in the world, the confluence of Washington's Blue Creek and the Cowlitz River is one such place. The mouth of the Methow River where it empties into the Columbia is another. In these locales and many others, the float offers such an obvious advantage that Northwest steelheaders have abandoned traditional bottom bouncing gear in favor of floats.

Many still water, or nearly still water, steelheading areas feature deep water and heavy concentrations of steelhead that may be holding well above the bottom. This is an ideal situation for the jig fishing steelheader.

Still water that is less than eight feet deep may be fished well with traditional fixed floats. However, often these quiet waters will run from 10 to 40 feet deep. These conditions call for a slip float. Drew covered rigging and casting slip floats on page 32. For now we will presume a complete understanding of the mechanics of slip float angling.

Still waters are best fished with light lines, small floats and lures that provide a strong visual stimuli without the benefit of movement provided by strong current flows. Light lines are necessary because clear water and slow moving lures give steelhead ample opportunity to examine our offering.

Small floats are used because there is no need for the buoyancy required to keep the float visible in choppy water. Another reason for small floats is their increased sensitivity. Still water steelhead often nibble delicately, so delicately the bite is barely discernible. Tiny floats will telegraph these tiny bites.

Almost any bait or lure will work beneath a still water float, but lures should be capable of providing an alluring action with no assistance from the current. Nothing does this better than marabou or rabbit fur. By far the most popular still water steelhead lure is the marabou jig.

Many still-water float fishers use an outfit something like this: An eight-foot rod designed for six to eight-pound test line, spinning reel filled

Floats and jigs have become very popular in still water areas such as Blue Creek on the Cowlitz River pictured here.

with six-pound line, a small slip float, and a one quarter or three eighths ounce marabou jig. Favorite jig colors are pink, pink and white, black and purple. Many experts use a small piece of shrimp meat on the hook of their jig to add flavor and scent. Others prefer a jig with a chenille or yarn body that they can soak in their favorite scent. Many excellent artificial scents are now marketed in liquid and paste form—favorite "flavors" include crawdad, shrimp and salmon eggs.

Still waters have little in the way of seams, riffles, or other surface markers to provide a hint as to what's beneath. But you can still do a bit of detective work to find the lay of the pool. As with moving water, you can use your float as a depth indicator. Simply keep lengthening the distance from float to lure until you know how deep the area is.

Steelhead in deep, still water are not always oriented with the bottom as is so common in flowing water. One day you may find the fish quite near the bottom of a 20-foot deep pool. The next day they may be near the bottom at the six foot depth and yet another day they will be suspended 10 feet deep in 20 feet of water. Trial and error, keen observation of others, and sharing of information with other anglers will help you learn what depth steelhead are at.

Even in relatively still water, subtle currents and wind will move your float. It's a good idea to keep your reel in free spool while applying slight tension on the spool with your thumb. Then let your float slowly slip down-

Dave Vedder shows a chrome-bright chum that fell for a pink jig fished beneath a dink float.

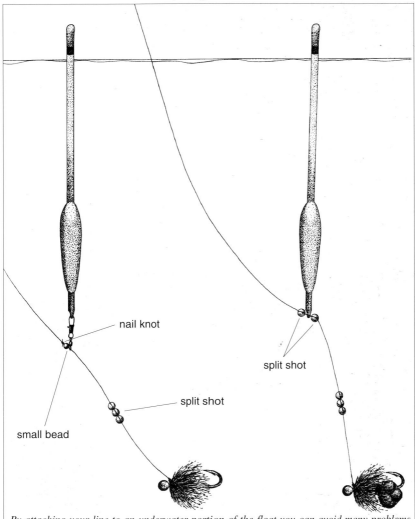

nail knot

split shot

split shot

small bead

By attaching your line to an underwater portion of the float you can avoid many problems caused by strong winds.

stream or as the wind dictates. If circumstances require an upstream cast, you will need to slowly retrieve line as the wind and current push the float back toward you. It is imperative that you keep all slack out of the line and watch your float like a hawk.

Strong wind can ruin your attempts to control the drift of your float and can make strike detection very difficult. There are, however, a few tricks to help you successfully battle the wind.

By using a float with a large mass beneath the water, you achieve a great deal of stability and you expose less surface to the wind. A float of the type illustrated lets you attach your line beneath the surface of the water. If winds are a big problem hold your rod tip beneath the water and keep all of your line from rod tip to the float submerged. This puts you in direct contact with the float with no line exposed to the wind. This trick will let you steer your float down wind then slowly bring it back with very little interference from the wind.

Still water steelhead often take the lure very gently. Often the pick-up is signaled by a slight lift of the float as the fish releases the tension on the line by mouthing the jig. Other times the only indication that a fish is present is a slight jiggling of your float. You must learn to strike very quickly when these tentative strikes occur. If you wait too long, the fish will drop the bait. If the float is lifting up, jiggling or, best of all, fully under water—strike!

If you miss the chance to strike, don't despair. Still-water steelhead often return to your jig as long as a bit of bait remains. This time be ready and strike the instant the float does anything that says "fish."

Still-water steelhead are affected by changes in barometric pressure, much like bass. When a cold front passes through with a dropping barometer, they often go off the bite or become very tentative biters. Fishing usually improves in stable weather.

Jig Fishing for Salmon

Drew Harthorn

To set the record straight, this is not about jigging for salmon with heavy lead jigs in the saltchuck. It's about adapting the use of a steelhead jig to catch salmon in the river.

The first, and certainly most important, aspect of catching a salmon in a river is to find a river that has salmon in it. The second most important aspect is going to the right location once you find said river. Is it by chance that anglers find holding areas that salmon like? No!

Unlike steelhead, salmon like the deep, cool, lazy water. Warm, fast, or shallow water drives them crazy. A textbook salmon hole in a river would be one with a steep cliff of either rock or clay on one side shaded by a lush covering of cedar, maple and fir trees, and between 15 and 20-feet deep. On the other side would be a little stream pouring its cool-running offering into the deep salmon hole. The type of hole just described is rare. What you need to find is a hole that has at least one or two of the described conditions. Then you'll be in business.

Jig fishing for salmon isn't the highest percentage technique that's out

there. Yet, there are times when it becomes very productive. Some Pacific salmon species are easier to catch using a jig than others. I'd have to say that based on previous experience, Chinook are about the hardest to fool. Humpies, on the other hand, are one of the easiest. Coho probably follow a close second to the humpies.

River salmon seem to key on scents. Chinook salmon are notorious for ignoring unscented lures and slamming lures that smell "right" to them. It is always a good idea to use a paste type scent on the head of marabou jigs or a liquid scent such as Dr. Juice Super Juice on jigs with absorbent bodies when salmon fishing. The scent will mask any human scent on your jig and may spell the difference between a bonanza day and a skunk.

Jig fishing for salmon is one of those "in your face" things. If the jig isn't put right in their face, they probably won't take it. I remember back to the fall of 1989 when the humpies were stacked as tight as cord wood in a deep hole in a small Hood Canal stream in Washington State. Most of the fish were tight to the bottom, but some were suspended. I immediately tied on one of Beau Mac's pink/white marabou steelhead jigs and floated it past the fish. The water was clear enough to see at least 30 feet in the hole. The jig passed a dozen fish before if floated right in the face of one fish. That fish slammed the jig so hard, it took my breath away. This same scenario was repeated about a half-dozen times until they wised up.

Two hours went by without a bite. A tactical change was necessary. The fish hovering near the bottom hadn't been at all interested until I took the float off and tied only the jig to the line. Bouncing a jig directly on the

Drew Harthorn shows a bright Olympic Peninsula chum that fell for a soft pink Beau Mac jig fished beneath a float.

Jig Fishing for Steelhead

bottom is risky at best. If you hang up, there goes the better part of two bucks. I hadn't made two or three casts, and it was fish on!

After releasing that fish, I started twitching the jig ever so slowly down the river bottom. The marabou tail of the jig was fluttering like a hula skirt on a Hawaiian dancer. It drove the fish crazy. Since observing that bunch of fish behaving in the way they did, I've fished jigs for salmon slow and deliberately.

To be effective with a suspended jig, finding the right water plays a big part. One of my favorite drifts is one that is three or four-feet deep along a brush covered or grassy bank. It's areas like these, provided the current is slow enough, coho, humpies, and chum salmon stack in. That ideal hole that I mentioned earlier is a good spring and fall Chinook hole.

With Chinook salmon being the glamour fish in the Northwest because of its size potential, you'll have to gear up to meet the strain these fish can put on your tackle: 15-pound test monofilament at a minimum. You can get away with lighter tackle for coho and humpies. Standard steelhead stuff will work just fine.

Time of day is also important. With the rivers having a tendency to run low and clear until the first rains hit in October, it's best to fish at first and last light. If it's at all possible, fish behind the fish. Salmon have a hard time seeing behind themselves. Floating a jig allows you to make a cast upstream 60 or 75 feet and have it drift right through the fish without getting hung up.

I'm going to leave the choice of jig color up to you as long as you start with pink for coho, humpies, and chums, and red for Chinook. An alternative color for coho, humpies, and chum would be a pink/white combination. From there it's your own personal choice.

One last tip is to fish with a barbless hook. I mentioned earlier the downfalls of fishing with a barbed hook. This is worth mentioning again. The hook has a lower chance of full penetration if the barb gets stuck near a bone. A hook that has only penetrated up to the barb has a high possibility of straightening out or simply falling out. Keep the hook sticky sharp and brace yourself.

Conclusion

Dave Vedder

If you follow the advice and instructions in this book, you will undoubtedly become more proficient at catching steelhead and river salmon. Drew and I fervently hope that you use this information to enhance your enjoyment of angling and not to stock your freezer. As

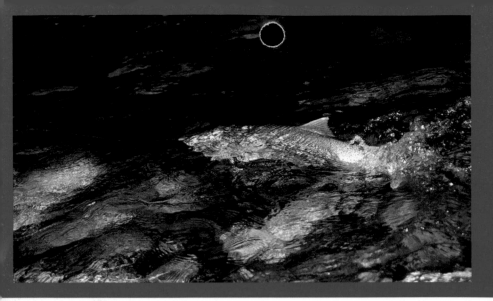

has become painfully clear in the 90s, no fishery can survive if today's huge population of anglers is allowed to kill all of the fish we catch.

Fortunately, the catch and release ethic is deeply imbedded in almost all serious steelheaders. I know of almost no serious steelheader who would kill a wild steelhead, even in those unenlightened backwaters where such practices are still legal. Yet, even these giant strides compared to where we were just a few years ago may not be enough.

Many recent studies have shown the steelhead mortality from catch and release angling may exceed seven percent. Such huge losses of wild steelhead are unacceptable. We must all strive to enjoy our fishery while doing as little damage as possible to the fish. To that end, we need to always pinch the barbs on our hooks, whether required by law or not. We must play our fish rapidly, and we must take the time to be sure the fish is rested and strong before we release it in gentle waters.

Even if we were to achieve the goal of 100 percent catch and release I suspect steelhead would continue to decline. Our rivers are plagued by outrageously destructive logging practices, a commercial fishing industry that has proven they have no regard for the resource, pollution, unchecked development and a host of other problems. If we want to assure that our grandchildren can enjoy the thrill of battling a leaping steelhead we must act today to protect our rivers.

There are dozens of worthy angling clubs and many other civic groups dedicated to protecting our rivers. It is not enough to wish them well. We must join the battle with our pocket books and our hearts. Join your local group of choice. Give them whatever financial support you can spare and give them some of your time. Our grandchildren will never forgive us if we stand by and let our wild steelhead and salmon disappear.

Winter steelheading at its finest.

Increase Your Steelhead Knowledge

To know all you need about steelhead fishing, subscribe to *Salmon Trout Steelheader* magazine. Each colorful issue is jam-packed with technique and location information about the greatest freshwater game fish of the Americas. If it's an effective new (or old) method of steelhead fishing, you'll find it in *STS*, along with great information about fishing for salmon and trout as well!

To subscribe call 1-800-541-9498, (503) 653-8108, Monday through Friday, Pacific Time, 8 am to 5 pm, or send a $19.95 check for the next six issues to: Frank Amato Publications, Inc., Box 82112, Portland, OR 97282. (Foreign and Canada add $5.00 per year, payable in U.S. Funds.)

Phone orders: 1-800-541-9498
Subscribe on the web: www.amatobooks.com